Guide to Quaker Practice

Howard H. Brinton

D0558476

PENDLE HILL PAMPHLET 20

Printed in the United States of America
by Sowers Printing Company, Lebanon, Pennsylvania
Twelfth printing March 1981/3,500

Contents

Suggested Bibliography

Friends for 300 Years, Howard H. Brinton; Harper & Row; Reprinted by Pendle Hill

Journal of John Woolman, Whittier Edition; Corinth Books (paper)

Journal of George Fox, Edited by Norman Penney; Dutton
Edited by John Nickalls; Cambridge

The Beginnings of Quakerism, William C. Braithwaite, Second Edition revised by Henry J. Cadbury; Cambridge

The Second Period of Quakerism, William C. Braithwaite, Second Edition revised by Henry J. Cadbury; Cambridge

Quakerism—A Spiritual Movement, Rufus M. Jones; Philadelphia Yearly Meeting

The Quakers—Their Story and Message, A. Neave Brayshaw; Allen and Unwin

The Story of Quakerism, Elfrida Vipont; Bannisdale

The Quaker Way of Life, William Wistar Comfort; American Friends Service Committee (paper)

The Faith and Practice of the Quakers, Rufus M. Jones; Philadelphia Yearly Meeting

Introduction

This *Guide*, originally written largely with new Friends' meetings in mind, has also met a considerable need in older meetings. It has been found to be useful not only as an aid to the instruction of new members but also as a reminder to older members of the character and significance of certain practices which at first sight may seem based only on custom or tradition. Books of Discipline issued by Yearly Meetings also serve this purpose but they necessarily contain in addition much technical information for the guidance of clerks of business meetings and other specific details. These are not necessary in a summary like this, which is written for a wider audience.

It should also be noted that this book contains information regarding many points on which Books of Discipline assume familiarity. Some customs have grown up so unobtrusively that they have not become matters of record. Accordingly, they may be entirely unknown to meetings composed largely of new members. Customs which have nothing but tradition to recommend them are intentionally omitted from this outline or mentioned only as matters of historical interest.

This seventh printing is required because of a continuing demand and by reason of rapidly changing conditions both without and within the Society of Friends. Old testimonies arise in new forms. For example, the testimony against oaths appears again today in connection with the new oaths of loyalty which may be the entering wedge in control of opinion by the state. Racial tensions, growing militarism, and increased fear of alien ideas demand from Friends new applications of old principles.

Within the Society of Friends growing unity solves many problems, but it also requires adjustment of divergent practices. Fortunately, most of these are slight. Their reconcilement needs little more than sufficient and correct information. As far as is practicable, this *Guide* supplies a summary based on Quaker practices as they existed prior to the appearance of divisions in the nineteenth century. Quaker practice went through a fluid period from 1650 to 1700 and became clearly formulated between 1700 and 1860. This book omits certain procedures in the meeting for worship which have been adopted in some areas since that time and which approximate practices prevailing in Protestant churches. The new meetings, for which this book was originally prepared, follow the older Quaker ways of worship. These meetings constitute the growing edge of Quakerism. More than two hundred new meetings have been set up during the past forty years. They will undoubtedly have much to contribute to some future *Guide to Quaker Practice*.

Methods of dealing with items which normally come before the meeting for business are outlined, but it is not intended that this summary serve as a substitute for a Book of Discipline issued by a Yearly Meeting.

H.H.B.

Practice and belief

This pamphlet is intended not as an interpretation of Quaker belief, but as a guide to Quaker practice. Yet practice presupposes belief. For this reason the determining principles of the Society of Friends must be kept constantly in mind.

Quaker beliefs are of two kinds—those which condition Christian behavior in general and are shared by other Christians, and those which give rise to unique practices. Within the present compass it will be possible to give attention only to the latter and to these only as they throw light on practice.

As a religious society, Friends have never officially issued statements of their beliefs comparable in authority to the written creeds of many other Christian bodies. Their reason for refraining from the formulation and use of creeds is the conviction that no form of words can adequately convey the living, growing truth of the Christian religion. This truth was first fully revealed in a Life lived on this earth. Truth of this kind continues to be revealed in and through life. In taking such an attitude as this toward creeds, the Society of Friends does not minimize the essential importance of the historical events which gave rise to the Christian revelation, nor does it underestimate the significance of the various interpretations and emphases which, in the nearly two thousand years of its history, the Christian Church has placed upon these events.

The New Testament as the first and most important of these interpretations is revered as a divine revelation of Truth, but it must be understood as a whole and not through isolated texts. The Spirit through which it was given forth continues to reveal Truth to the human heart. It is only through this Spirit that the whole meaning of the New Testament can be grasped. When so grasped it becomes a guide to practice and belief.

The customary procedures of the Society of Friends might be compared to the typical procedures of scientists. Scientific societies admit to their membership only those who are qualified to use, and willing to use, the scientific method. The basis of the test is not facts arrived at but the method used. Scientists may disagree on facts, but they do not disagree on method. Similarly the Society of Friends accepts into membership a person who is willing to follow the Quaker method regardless of where it may lead. But every method is based on some definite belief. The scientist bases his method on the theory that the universe is a cosmos not a chaos and that under similar conditions the same causes will produce the same results. The Quaker bases his method on belief in a God-centered spiritual universe, the inner truth and meaning of which is in some degree accessible to man. Without definite underlying beliefs neither the scientist nor the Quaker would expect that those who follow the same methods would arrive at the same conclusions. The analogy can be carried a step further. As scientists agree on a certain well established body of scientific facts inherited from the research and discovery of the past and subject to continual revision, so the Quakers have accepted a certain body of religious and social doctrines inherited from the past and subject always to new interpretations as more Truth is apprehended.

Tested and established practices in a religious society are as important as are good habits for an individual. Yet such practices must not become so fixed that they are no longer subject to improvement and growth. During the eighteenth century the Society of Friends in America was a highly disciplined body with a sharply defined cultural pattern. During this period it grew and prospered. In the latter part of the nineteenth century and even more in the twentieth, partly as a result of the reaction against authoritarian tendencies which had resulted in divisions and partly as a result of the broadening effect of higher education, Quakerism to many persons became almost synonymous with an attitude of toleration toward all practices and opinions. Neither the severe discipline of the eighteenth century nor the laxity of the early twentieth will meet the need of today. A religious group which has a definite character and yet is open to new incursions of Truth is in a better position than one which stresses outworn traditions or one which so neglects the wisdom of the past embodied in inherited customs as to have become like a man without a memory.

The positive usually prevails over the negative, and the group which adheres to a well-defined and well-grounded way of life has an advantage over one whose character is vague and formless. A river confined within its banks has more power and depth than one which spreads over a plain.

The meeting for worship

Meetings function in two capacities, for worship and for business. The meeting gathers to wait upon God at least once a week, preferably oftener. Worship is central and fundamental in Quaker practice. Out of it all other religious and social exercise is derived. In the form here described, this is the only practice of the Society of Friends which has existed from the start without going through a process of development. Its discovery was the discovery of Quakerism. The form of Quaker worship first arose not from theory but from experience. The early Friends discovered the Divine Presence in their hearts at a time when current religion consisted largely in belief in a distant God and His plan of salvation as recorded in a sacred book. They accepted much of the theology of their time, giving it their own interpretation, but they added one important element, namely, direct contact with the Divine Source from which had sprung the Sacred Book itself. This Source of Life and Truth was called the "Light Within," "Christ Within," "that of God in every man," "the Seed of the Kingdom." Although this doctrine finds expression in John's gospel and letters, Paul's epistles, and the writings of the Christian mystics, the Quakers of the 17th century believed that they had become aware of it directly by their own experience of the Light. For them religion could no longer be a matter of words, doctrines and ritual. It was communion with Divinity itself, speaking with the very voice of Him who once spoke in Galilee.

This Light was the Word of God, the Way, the Truth, and the Life, the Eternal Christ. Therefore it "lighteth every man that cometh into the world." There was evidence of its operation in the works of pre-Christian philosophers and un-Christian Mohammedans. It was not to be confused with human reason and human conscience. Being above both, it is that whereby reason becomes more enlightened and conscience becomes more sensitized. It is the Absolute Value which is the source of all relative values, however imperfectly it may be comprehended by the human understanding. It is that Creative Power which first dawned on chaos and which draws all things upward into nobler states of being. It is also warm, living, and personal, forever pleading with man to give up his selfish doing and desiring, and follow its Divine Leading.

Three main functions belong to the Light—it affords

knowledge of religious truth and moral values, it supplies power whereby man derives strength to act on this knowledge, and it enables men to achieve cooperation and unity among themselves. As source of truth it gives guidance and particularly brings about awareness of sin and shortcoming; as source of power it enables weak, average human beings to do great things; as source of unity it causes the whole meeting to act as one person. In Quaker literature the phrase "joined to the Lord" is frequently followed by the correlative phrase "and to one another."

To believe that there is in man that which is more than himself, through which he is lifted up beyond himself, is by no means peculiar to Quakerism or even to Christianity. What is peculiar is the type of religious worship based entirely on this experience, yet not divorced from Christian concepts. Such worship is not sermon-centered as in Protestantism, nor altar-centered as in Catholicism; but centered in the Divine Life flowing into and through human hearts whereby we commune with God.

The meeting quietly assembles at the appointed hour. Members should gather without conversation. Late-comers are sources of disturbance. The "service" begins when the worshiper begins to serve. Each one sits in expectant silence, his soul reaching upwards.

The Society of Friends has never issued specific instructions regarding what the worshiper should do during the silence, believing that such instruction would limit the freedom of the Spirit which, like the wind, "bloweth where it listeth." Sufficient for many is the admonition so often heard in Quaker meetings: "Heed the intimations within." The way of true worship can eventually be found though it may sometimes require devout and patient search.

Friends do not use visible Sacraments of Baptism and Communion because they endeavor to seek directly the inward Reality of which these are outward symbols. To those who hold that the sacraments have more than a symbolic value, Friends reply that outward observances cannot carry more of Divine grace than is found in the inward baptism of the Spirit and inner communion with God. Any event in life is sacramental if it is truly an outward evidence of inward grace.

For similar reasons, Friends do not sing hymns nor recite prayers in their meetings for worship because, when this is done, words are uttered for which there may be no corresponding personal experience. Words, whether sung or spoken, should, in this most important of all exercises, be the spontaneous outward expression of an immediate inner condition. This is seldom the case when the form of words is prescribed in advance.

The spiritual practice which the worshiper finds most profitable during the silence will depend upon the problem he is facing and upon his own condition. He will sometimes find himself led mysteriously, apparently without his volition, from one kind of spiritual exercise to another. Often it is better simply to disregard wandering thoughts rather than to attempt to suppress them, to "look over their shoulders," as we are advised by the unknown author of the Cloud of Unknowing. While the surface of the mind may be ruffled with passing winds of thought or fantasy the deeper regions may at the same time be active in prayer and worship. It is, however, best for the mind to be kept under control.

A part of worship can be compared to climbing a hill and another part to the view from the summit. In the first, man is active, in the second, passive; in the first, the mind is busy with many thoughts, in the second, the mind is stilled so that light can break in from beyond the horizon of self-conscious thought. The following spiritual exercises are among the possibilities which may present themselves in the preliminary more self-activating part of worship.

Self-examination. This important exercise is placed first because it may be the means by which the worshiper discovers what intervenes between himself and a deeper communion with God. The obstacle may be a selfish or degrading desire, or merely a mind too busy with routine affairs. As awareness of human limitation progresses, less is seen with human eyes and more with the eyes of God. The inner vision is thereby enlarged to include not only the worshiper but those around him and others through wider and wider reaches in the world outside.

Repeating to oneself a passage from the Bible or some devotional poem or other words and reflecting on their meaning. Here there must be an effort to come into that Spirit out of which the words came, for only in the Light of that Spirit can the words have life and power.

Reviewing in imagination some event in one's own life, in history or in the life of Christ, with reflection upon its significance.

Prayer with words that have been learned.

Prayer with one's own words and thoughts, including confession and thanksgiving.

Such prayers are not merely petitions. They are more like communion with friend or lover when inmost desire is exposed in the light of another presence. As prayer gains in power and inwardness it becomes more and more simplified until it culminates in that which overtops all the complexities of thought.

Then there may follow *Prayer without words,* an upsurge of feeling and will toward God. Such prayer cannot remain long in a condition of striving. It should pass over into quiet waiting and obedience. Activity is replaced by expectant passivity in which there may arise a sense of God's nearness. As that sense increases the worshiper feels his own will drawn into harmony with a Greater Will.

Such exercises of self-examination, memory, imagination and prayer are not to be sharply distinguished from one another because the whole person may very well be present in all of them. On a given occasion, they may or may not fit the condition of the worshiper. His path does not lie over a well-marked road, for in worship he is on the frontier of his conscious being. Such explicit exercises belong primarily in the area of man's upward tending toward God rather than in the realm of God's reach toward man, though there is a sense in which we cannot seek for God without, in some degree, having already found him.

Prayer, as it becomes freed from words and thoughts, imperceptibly passes over from man's out-reach toward God to God's answer to man. The restless, fragmentary human will finds itself centered in a deeper, wider Will in which it is fulfilled and at peace. The soul is filled with the sense of Divine Presence. All is suffused with Light and Power. Awareness of self fades out and only God remains.

Such experience is seldom attained by struggling for it. It may dawn suddenly and unexpectedly even without our asking, or, again, it may occur so simply and naturally as to be passed over lightly, its significance being recognized only in retrospect. God is not in the fire and the earthquake, the spectacular and the thrilling, but in the still, small voice. He may come as quietly and unexpectedly as Christ came to Palestine, the Christ who said to Philip, "Have I been so long time with you and yet hast thou not known me?" Every human being is capable of an experience of God though he may not give the experience a name.

The autobiographies of Friends nearly all report intervening periods of dryness when God seems far away and the very meeting for worship itself is formal and unfruitful. Almost everyone passes through such stages which should not become times of too deep discouragement. Drought is eventually followed by refreshing rain. After such seasons the new life may be as small as the germ within a seed. Growth should not be hurried. The slower the growth the longer-lived the plant.

To the surface of the mind with which we meet the world around us, worship adds the dimension of depth. Friends speak of "centering down" in a meeting, meaning that the focus of attention should be placed in those profound regions where the ultimate meaning of life is discovered. Here the longing of the individual worshiper is no longer the center of interest, not because it is wholly eliminated, but because it finds itself transformed by being organically related to a larger whole of life which has no outer limit. Such an achievement is especially important to the intellectual man who is often one-sided and specialized because he is so exclusively concerned with the rationalizing, analyzing area of the mind. Through these preoccupations he becomes unaware of his roots in the deep, spiritual soil of his existence. To him silent worship offers one essential ingredient of life that cannot be obtained through books, lectures, or sermons. It is no accident that most of the newer Friends' meetings have grown up around colleges and universities because they supply that which is not practiced in any college course.

After worship comes action. The history of the Society of Friends shows that the spiritual exercises of the meeting do not, as a rule, result in attempts to escape from the world but rather in efforts to emend it. Yet worship is an end in itself, for God is not known in order that He may be used. Nevertheless we know that we have been with Him if our reason has been enlightened, our conscience sensitized and our will set in the right direction. The experience which lifts us out of the world carries us back into it for we cannot know the joy and peace of God without seeking to bring that joy and peace to others. The worshiper finds that he is a creature both of eternity and of time, of the Kingdom of God and of this Earth. Realization of the eternal brings him inner peace and serenity, but there follows, without disturbing this peace, a sense of contrast between the two realms. The worshiper then discovers that he must set about changing something in the realm of earth that it may more closely approximate the Kingdom of God. To do this he must himself act as far as he is able as a member of the Divine Kingdom. Out of such considerations and such experiences arise the social testimonies of the Society of Friends.

Preparation for worship

The success of meetings for worship depends to some extent on preparation during intervening times, and especially the period immediately preceding the meeting. This is not a conscious and deliberate preparation for a specific time and place, but a general preparation of life and character. The mystics in all ages have told us that a good moral character is a prerequisite for the highest religious experiences. Anger, hatred, greed, jealousy, and snobbishness are barriers. The appropriate type of character has sometimes been sought through ascetic practices affording training in self-control. But life usually provides enough unsought experiences to enable us to give practice to our wills in controlling and inhibiting our lower desires and in stimulating good impulses. Worship requires self-control and the ability to concentrate on the highest. If some act during the week has opened a chasm between the soul and God, explicit efforts must be made to bridge this gulf. The spanning is never solely the work of man.

One important type of preparation for group worship is individual devotion. A daily period of prayer, worship, and meditation furnishes food for the nourishment of spiritual life. So also does regular reading of devotional literature. Sometimes a meeting is helped if a small group meets occasionally for preparation through worship together.

The time immediately preceding First Day morning meeting is important in preparing for the period of worship. Quiet reading of appropriate books may be helpful. The Sunday morning newspaper is a poor form of preparation. Animated discussion in a First Day School class may so ruffle up the surface of the mind that it will take a considerable period of time to restore that degree of quiet which makes worship possible. A forum or First Day School should accordingly be held after the meeting for worship rather than before. In this way, instead of the meeting for worship being infected with the spirit of discussion, the discussion will be infused with the spirit of worship.

The spoken word

The spiritual exercises of the meeting may include spoken words. No one should go to a Friends' meeting with the definite expectation either of speaking or of not speaking. Each attender should be open to dealing appropriately with whatever may be laid upon him by the Spirit of Truth and Life.

It is no light matter to break the living silence. This should be done only with a sense of humility. Spoken words should not come as an interruption of the silence but rather as a component part of it. The tone of voice and manner of the speaker must harmonize with the character of the meeting.

As the worshiper sits in silence some message may arise out of the depth of his soul which he recognizes by its nature to be intended not simply for himself but for the gathering as a whole. If he does not express it, he finds himself burdened with a sense of omission, but if he faithfully utters it there follows a sense of clearness and relief.

This peculiar sense of urgency is usually the sign of divine requirement. There is no sure, no single test of guidance. The sensitive person learns to recognize the call as clearly as he recognizes the voice of his friend. He knows his friend's voice even though he may be quite unable to describe its quality. A clear conviction that the need of the meeting or of some persons in it or even that one's own need requires that words be uttered is often the only assurance when there is doubt. Though a message may seem intellectually fitting it should not be given unless it glows with life.

In such matters as these no rules can or ought to be given. The following characteristics of an acceptable spoken message are suggested as possibly valid in most cases. Seldom does a speaker achieve them all, but, fortunately, God is willing to use very imperfect instruments to accomplish His purposes. The sermon should be—

• *Religious.* There is no limitation on the subject of the sermon, but, whatever the subject, it must be conceived in a religious rather than a secular manner. The difference between the religious and secular defies definition though most persons can recognize it. As in mathematics a geometrical figure may have certain characteristics if it appears in one system of reference and other characteristics in another system of reference, so the same theme may have different connotations in a religious reference from those which it exhibits in a secular reference. In the religious focus one endeavors to see the matter as God would see it rather than as man would see it. Solemnity of utterance and reverence of bearing strengthen the religious nature of the message. An academic discussion of economic problems would interfere with the spirit of worship, but a solemn, reverent appeal for greater sensitivity of conscience in economic matters might deepen the meeting. Speakers who persist in giving the meeting messages of a non-religious character can be afforded an opportunity to speak at times other than the meeting for worship if what they have to say is profitable.

• *Spontaneous.* The spoken message is not prepared in advance of the meeting. It grows up, sometimes as unexpectedly as a green sprout from the soil. This does not mean that there is no preparation for the ministry, but that such preparation secures general fitness, not explicit preparation for a special occasion. It sometimes happens that a definite message grows slowly; in such a case it should not be delivered until it has reached sufficient maturity. This process may require many days or months. If a message arises in the mind outside of the meeting for worship it must be kept until there is a clear feeling that the appropriate time has arrived to give it utterance.

• *Non-personal.* One who utters a message in a Friends' meeting should think of himself as an instrument through whom the Spirit speaks. He must eliminate himself as much as possible in order that what is greater than himself may flow through him. This spoken message bears no similarity to the kind of self-exposure characteristic of the so-called "experience meeting."

• *Non-argumentative.* The speaker does not argue. He states simply and directly a message which he believes will be recognized as true by its very character. This was the method of Jesus. The Quaker vocal utterance should never take on the quality which belongs to the public address, the forum or lecture hall.

• *Simple.* It is an ancient testimony of Friends that persons not formally educated are quite as likely to be called to the service of the ministry as are the academically trained. The simplicity of the gospel may be obscured by learned discourse and elaborate discussion. There is nothing in our religion which cannot be fully grasped by the simple-minded. Nevertheless, God can do more with a good instrument than a defective one, and life-long self-education, if given its right place, undoubtedly increases effectiveness, supplying a wider range of expressions and illustrations without destroying the simplicity of the message. All unusual words and oratorical flourishes should be discouraged. The person who speaks glibly may need to be deepened.

• *Brief.* Only a very few persons can today successfully deliver long sermons in a Friends' meeting. Usually a message can be fully given within a few minutes. Often a single sentence, spoken with reverence and conviction, carries more weight than do many words. There should be no fear that too much of the meeting will be held in silence. A visiting Friend who is seldom heard may naturally be expected to occupy more time than a local Friend who is often heard. A brief message uttered early in the meeting may help some whose thoughts have been wandering to focus attention on a single subject.

• *Unified, with itself, and other utterances.* The speaker rises with a certain concern; when his mind has been unburdened he weakens the effect if he passes on to other matters. The ability to cease when the message, however brief, has been delivered is a valued accomplishment.

A meeting is generally the better if the several messages bear some relation to one another. This helps to gather the meeting into a spirit of unity. A rapid change of tenor is disconcerting and should never occur except after a suitable interval. Here also no rules can be given which might limit the freedom of the Spirit. It may be important that a new subject be brought before the meeting.

The value of the utterance depends quite as much upon

the listener as upon the speaker. Sometimes the hearer loses help which he might have received had he been sympathetic and sensitive instead of critical and hardened. If a speaker is difficult to tolerate, he presents nevertheless a real opportunity for the cultivation of forbearance.

Friends with a concern to speak who belong to a meeting where there is much speaking do well to visit meetings where there is a dearth of ministry.

It is not the custom among Friends to commend a speaker, since speaking in meeting is considered to be the work of God and not man. The message, not the messenger, is important. Nevertheless a speaker may receive needed encouragement by learning that his message has helped someone. He may also be encouraged if he finds that the thought which he expressed is developed further by a subsequent speaker.

Vocal prayer

The spirit of prayer arising in the heart of the worshiper may find vocal utterance. When a person so "appears in supplication," to use a once common Quaker phrase, he becomes the mouthpiece of the whole assembly which prays to God through him. He does not say "I" but "we" for private petition is presented in silence. In earlier times Friends felt it natural that there should be vocal prayer near the beginning and near the end of the meeting. Many today feel that the best prayer is wordless, yet there is no doubt that sincere and deeply felt utterance addressed briefly and directly to the Most High adds power to a meeting.

Because timidity and awe are for some natures too overpowering, Friends are cautioned to be patient with themselves and with one another and to endeavor here also to perfect the instrument, or to allow it, through divine ministration, to become perfected, so as to be capable of adequately conveying the words of grace. In the vocal expression of adoration, thanksgiving, penitence and petition, thought and feeling are so united that the deeper sources of religious life are drawn upon.

The absence of aptitude for every sort of prophetic utterance is a characteristic of our time. It results from our shying away from the deeper mysteries of existence in favor of regions scientifically understood.

In former times the person appearing in supplication knelt and the congregation stood. Today the congregation generally remains seated and the person offering prayer kneels or stands, or, in an informal meeting, such as that of a work camp, he may remain seated like the others.

Timing the meeting

Both eternity and time have their proper connection with worship, and this is true despite the fact that the best in worship is achieved when the worshiper is unconscious of the passage of time, and is not reminded of it by a clock.

The suitable duration of a meeting is judged not by a predetermined number of hours or minutes but by the judgment of two responsible Friends who shake hands when they feel that the meeting has been brought to a conclusion. In most meetings one person is looked upon as sitting at the head of the meeting; his responsibility is to time it. He is not usually selected by any formal process, it being generally obvious who is qualified. In some meetings the elders or the committee on ministry and counsel assign this duty to a suitable person. A meeting should never be timed by a visiting Friend.

In recent years the First Day morning meeting for worship has tended to last about one hour. In earlier generations it often continued for two or three hours or longer. The steadily decreasing length of the period of public worship is a sign of decreasing spiritual vitality. An hour should be considered a minimum for a weekly meeting. It is seldom that the best in worship can be fully developed or attained in a shorter time. For daily meetings a shorter period may be expected.

Physical environment

Worship may be affected by physical environment, though this is not necessarily the case. The room should be of satisfying size and proportion. It should be plain, including only necessary equipment. Friends' meeting houses built during the 18th century are often excellent examples of proportion and simplicity. Attention should be paid to heat, light, and ventilation. The earliest Friends' meetings, like the gatherings of the early Christians, were held in homes and many valued meetings for worship are still so held. Others convene in places not specifically built for the purpose. Friends should not be scattered about, but should gather in an orderly manner comparatively near to one another, though not crowded. This helps to produce a feeling of unity. Strangers should be shown to appropriate seats. Assembling in an orderly fashion and sitting in a decorous manner has real importance for this highest human endeavor. Outward slouching detracts from the likelihood of inner concentration. Even in work camps and other places where the exigencies of space and the absence of chairs require sitting on the ground, a certain orderliness and erect posture should be maintained.

The seating arrangements of meeting houses are of two types, each presenting its own peculiar advantages. The type which was universal till recent times consisted of two or three rows of raised benches along the longer side of the room facing the other benches. The raised seats were called "facing benches" or "the gallery." They were occupied by the older and more experienced Friends. Persons "in the body of the meeting" might be invited to sit in these seats by elders or overseers. An advantage of this arrangement is that those most likely to appear in the ministry are seated in a position in which they can best be heard. Another advantage is that the beginner in worship can see before him examples of persons who, having progressed further than himself, show in their countenances the effect of this further progress. In the second type of arrangement, which has been adopted by most of the newer meetings, the seats are drawn up in a hollow square or circle. One side may be left open for a fire place. This arrangement seems to many to be more democratic and more likely to inculcate an even distribution of the sense of responsibility.

Other historical types of meetings

Two early types of Friends' meetings should be considered briefly. The *retired meeting* was held "in the pure silence of all flesh." Little or no speaking seems to have been expected. It was small and secluded, sometimes held early on a First Day morning in the second story of the Meeting House. Those went to it who desired relief from excess of speaking in the larger meeting.

The *threshing meeting* was held with the express purpose of convincing people of the doctrines of the Society of Friends. It was addressed by so-called "public Friends" who, often with Bible in hand, used all their powers of utterance to convince their hearers of *the Truth*. Reports of these meetings indicate that they included long periods of silent waiting. The name "threshing meetings" arose from the purpose of the preacher "to separate the wheat from the chaff." Friends who were convinced at such meetings were directed to the regular meetings for worship. There, in the silence, the more fundamental and sometimes long process of conversion would take place.

A frequent type of informal meeting was called "an opportunity." The term was generally used to designate a meeting for worship which began suddenly and unexpectedly in a group assembled for social or other purposes. The group, noticing the silence and gravity of one of its members, became silent. A verbal communication or prayer was generally given followed by a period of silence. After that the conversation was resumed. Sometimes there was more prearrangement. A Friend might ask for "an opportunity" in a home or school. This meant that he desired to hold a brief and informal meeting there and perhaps, during the silence, unburden himself of some communication which he had on his mind to give. Family visiting, during which a brief meeting for worship would, as a rule, be held, was once a highly important element in Quaker practice.

Another religious exercise of great historical importance was the daily reading of the Bible in the family. The reading was followed by a brief period of silence. This practice was once almost universal among Friends, and the subject of yearly inquiry by the meeting.

Eldership

Very early in the Quaker movement it was recognized that certain Friends were qualified to have more responsibility than others for the good order of the meeting. This was urgent in the early days when the movement was fluid, without definite membership, and when fanatics of all sorts were going about claiming to have part in it. Stable personalities with a gift for curbing extravagances or encouraging the weak were appointed for these duties and were called Elders. At first some of them were ministers as well, but later the functions of minister and elder were differentiated. Still later, the elders themselves became divided into two groups exercising two types of pastoral care, one retaining the title of elders, whose special responsibility was the spiritual vitality of the meeting for worship and the other with the name overseers who exercised care over the moral conduct of the membership and performed various formal duties.*

Elders, or their equivalent, are still appointed by most meetings. In one group of Yearly Meetings their functions are performed by "Committees on Ministry and Counsel."† Elders, or members of this Committee, are appointed by the Monthly Meeting, their names being presented to the meeting by a nominating committee. Such a nominating committee must recognize that eldership, like the ministry, is a gift bestowed by the Spirit, not an office to be passed around. In some meetings no elders exist because no one is felt to have a gift for this service. Such spiritual advisors for the meeting should be persons of tact and discernment who naturally draw to them those in need of help.

The duties of elders are mainly concerned with promoting conditions favorable to the success of the meeting for worship. Their special concern is the ministry. They should be qualified to advise those who speak in meeting, encouraging a ministry which is helpful and rightly based and discouraging whatever is distracting and gives evidence of having arisen from a mistaken zeal. If the elders feel that certain members are withholding what should be given to the meeting or are not diligent in developing their gifts, they should offer encouragement. They must also deal firmly with persons who abuse the freedom of the meeting with long and burdensome discourse.

For many years in the Society of Friends elders and ministers whose gift in the ministry had been "recorded" or "recognized" in the minutes of the meeting for business, met

---

* For duties of overseers, see p. 38.

† In the Philadelphia Discipline of 1955 they are called the "Meetings on Worship and Ministry."

together at regular intervals to consider the spiritual life of the meeting. The older ministers advised the younger and the elders advised both. Such meetings of ministers and elders are still continued in some areas.

Structure

The unit in the Society of Friends is not the individual member or family, but the meeting, which consists of a group of persons who convene at regular times to wait upon God and for the purpose of transacting their corporate business. Such a meeting is free to undertake any activity that can better be accomplished by a group than by an individual. This basic unit is generally called a Monthly Meeting because its official sessions for transacting business are held monthly, though, when need arises, the meeting may convene by special appointment at briefer intervals. Sometimes the Monthly Meeting is divided into two or more meetings called Preparative Meetings, but the Monthly Meeting to which the Preparative Meetings belong and in which they meet together once a month, still remains the fundamental executive unit. Membership in the Society of Friends exists only through membership in a particular Monthly Meeting.

Just as an individual member is, as it were, a cell in the larger organic entity which is the Monthly Meeting, so this meeting may itself occupy a similar place in a larger structure, the Quarterly Meeting, which may in its turn be a like constituent part of a still more inclusive whole, the Yearly Meeting. Thus each Yearly Meeting is composed of Quarterly Meetings and each Quarterly Meeting of Monthly Meetings. Membership in the Monthly Meeting includes membership in the Quarterly Meeting and Yearly Meeting.

Individual members have the same rights and responsibilities in the larger groups to which they belong as in the

27

smaller group. Although representatives are sometimes appointed to the larger groups from the smaller, this is done to make sure that the smaller is represented in the larger meeting. Such representatives have no authority or privileges not possessed by other members who attend the larger meeting. A concern, that is, a strong sense of some special requirement based on religious insight, may originate with an individual member and, after being communicated by him to the Monthly Meeting may, if circumstances require it, and if the Monthly Meeting approves, be sent up by the Monthly Meeting to the Quarterly Meeting and then, if need be, and if the Quarterly Meeting approves, from the Quarterly Meeting to the Yearly Meeting for consideration and action. The individual may, if he desires, express his concern directly to the Quarterly or Yearly Meeting. In this way undertakings needing support of a group larger than that which exists in the Monthly Meeting may secure backing. The larger groups function as do the smaller groups.

After the separations which occurred in the Society of Friends in America during the nineteenth century, the Yearly Meetings, with some exceptions, formed several loosely cohering groups popularly designated as branches. Today, however, the American situation is even more complex. Some Monthly Meetings belong, as a whole, to two Yearly Meetings of different branches, some have a membership which is partly in one Yearly Meeting, partly in another and partly in both, and some, which include members of a variety of Yearly Meetings or of no Yearly Meeting, are independent. Some meetings have as yet no enrolled membership and are not organized for conducting business. A few groups of independent meetings have formed Associations which fulfill many of the functions of a Yearly Meeting. This fluidity in the present organization of the Society of Friends is a sign of growth and development, and an evidence that many of the old branch distinctions are no longer important. As long as the Monthly Meeting remains the fundamental unit, the more inclusive groupings can be made up in a variety of ways. Such conditions, due to the fact that new meetings generally contain members from a variety of Quaker groups, are probably temporary and transitional. It is expected that, wherever and whenever possible, the older normal arrangement will be established which existed before the separations. In many areas these separations have ceased to exist.

The larger bodies, such as Quarterly and Yearly Meetings, do not exist to exert authority over the Monthly Meetings, but rather to undertake such matters as cannot so well be undertaken by the smaller bodies. They serve to overcome the isolation of the smaller groups by linking them to a larger whole with its correspondingly greater breadth and variety of view, its more inclusive range of acquaintanceship, and its greater power to carry out certain concerns. The reasons why a Monthly Meeting should join a larger body are similar, in some respects, to the reasons why an individual should join a Monthly Meeting. The union of smaller units to form larger groups need not take place upon a geographical basis. It may more properly take place on a basis of congeniality and similarity of views and practices.

The Yearly Meeting issues to Monthly Meetings Queries, Advices, and reports of its proceedings. It also requests money for the support of its enterprises. Monthly Meetings report to Quarterly Meetings and Quarterly Meetings to Yearly Meetings. The authority of the larger meetings over their constituent meetings is not infrequently confined to the following two points: (1) a Monthly Meeting can be set up or laid down only by the authority of a Quarterly Meeting. Similarly a Quarterly Meeting can be set up or laid down only by the authority of a Yearly Meeting. And (2) an individual disciplined in a lower meeting can appeal for further consideration of his case to a higher meeting. Books of Discipline (or of Faith and Practice), issued by Yearly Meetings, contain regulations for the use of meetings for business.

A Monthly Meeting may be very small and yet fully able to fulfill all its functions. There is some difference of opinion regarding the maximum size beyond which a meeting can operate in a satisfactory manner. Probably when the average attendance is much beyond fifty, two meetings should be formed out of the one. When such a division takes place care should be taken that each group contains the same variety in age and experience.

Until recently Friends kept no statistical records of membership as they considered that growth or decline could not be estimated in terms of numbers. The fact that as few as two or three persons can constitute a meeting for worship gives to Friends an advantage in setting up new meetings not possessed by religious groups whose manner of worship makes more elaborate requirements.

New meetings sometimes spring up spontaneously when two or more persons feel the need of silent worship together. As others discover this meeting and sense the life in it, the meeting will grow. After a time this group will feel the need of strengthening which comes from association with other like-minded groups. Some new meetings grow up from the very beginning under the care of an established Monthly Meeting of Friends. These, before they become regularly organized, are called Indulged Meetings or Allowed Meetings.

Meeting for business

Every meeting should hold a business session at least once a month. This should be preceded by a time of worship in order that the spirit of worship may pervade the transaction of business. In both the meeting for worship and the meeting for business, guidance is sought from the Spirit of Truth and Life by whose operation the group is brought into love and unity.

It might appear at first sight that the principles of Quakerism are inconsistent with any form of church government. This would be true if each individual is expected to follow his own insight regardless of the insight of others. Such individualism could readily result in religious anarchism. This view had considerable following when Quakerism began. It was called "Ranterism." Many Ranters who had become Friends left the Society when its system of church government was set up. Quakerism is not anarchistic. The principle of corporate guidance, according to which the Spirit can inspire the group as a whole, is central. Since there is but one Truth, its Spirit, if followed, will produce unity. To achieve this unity is always possible and the Society of Friends has practised the method of achieving it with considerable success for three centuries.

In the transaction of business the meeting assumes that it will be able to act as a unit. No vote is ever taken. If a high degree of unity cannot be reached, the meeting does not act. The only necessary official is a clerk whose business it is to apprehend and record the sense of the meeting. The deliberations of this type of meeting are notably different from procedure by parliamentary rules.

Gathering the sense of the meeting

The business before the meeting is generally presented by the clerk, but it may come through a committee report or from an individual speaking under a sense of concern. The members of the meeting should freely express their opinions regarding the action which they think should be taken. By listening to these expressions the clerk seeks to gather the sense or opinion of the meeting as a whole. When the discussion has reached a stage that indicates that the meeting is arriving at a fair degree of unity, the clerk, or his assistant, prepares a minute which states the judgment at which he thinks the meeting has arrived. The minute is read, either immediately after the decision is made or at the close of the meeting, the former being the historical practice which is still followed in some areas. Corrections or additions may be suggested by members at large. The minute is not valid until it has been both read to the meeting and approved by it. Modern minutes sometimes include not only decisions, but also a summary of reports and discussions. Such minutes are often too elaborate to be prepared during the meeting of which they are a record.

On routine affairs little or no discussion may be necessary, and the clerk may assume that silence gives consent. In such matters the clerk may prepare his minute before the meeting begins, but it must in any case be read and approved in the course of the meeting. On matters which require it, time should be allowed for members to deliberate and to express themselves fully. A variety of opinions may be voiced until someone arises and states an opinion which meets with general approval. This agreement is signified by the utterance of such expressions as "I agree," "I approve," "That Friend speaks my mind." If a few are still unconvinced they may nevertheless remain silent or withdraw their objections in order that this item of business may be completed, but if they remain strongly convinced of the validity of their opinion and state that they are not able to withdraw the objection, the clerk generally feels unable to make a minute. In gathering the sense of the meeting the clerk must take into consideration that some Friends have more wisdom and experience than others and their conviction should therefore carry greater weight. The opposition of such Friends cannot, as a rule, be disregarded. Chronic objectors must be dealt with considerately, even though their opinions may carry little weight.

If a strong difference of opinion exists on a matter on which decision cannot be postponed, the subject may be referred to a small special committee with power to act, or else to a standing committee of the meeting. Often an urgent appeal by the clerk or by some other Friend to obstructive persons will cause them to withdraw their objections. It must be remembered, however, that minorities are sometimes right. When a serious state of disunity exists and feelings become aroused, the clerk or some other Friend may ask the meeting to sit for a time in silence in the spirit of worship. The effect of this quiet waiting is often powerful in creating unity.

Theoretically the clerk is not a presiding but a recording officer. However, the situation is often such that he must become in some sense a moderator, as for instance when two persons rise to speak at once. Under other circumstances recognition from him is not necessary in order to gain the floor. A clerk's most difficult problem is to determine the right speed with which business can be satisfactorily transacted. He must wait for a full expression of opinion, but he should not allow the procedure to lag, especially if there is a great deal of business to be transacted. Sometimes he must encourage Friends to express themselves. Experience will acquaint him with the subtler aspects of his task; on how much vocal expression and on whose judgment he can most wisely base his minute and on what kinds of questions complete unity may or may not be essential.

The clerk is responsible for seeing that only one subject is discussed at a time. The meeting is at liberty to change the subject, but it is the clerk's duty to keep discussion to the subject in hand until the meeting itself has decided to shift it. He must also remind Friends regarding items of unfinished business. He must ask a speaker who addresses an individual to address the meeting as a whole. If a speaker is not easily heard or understood the clerk may repeat his remarks to the meeting. If someone takes up too much time, the clerk or some other Friend may feel it right to ask him to conclude his remarks.

Sometimes, and this is peculiarly necessary in large gatherings, the clerk may be helped by one or more assistant clerks in reading reports and in drawing up minutes. The record may, if desired, include a brief summary of discussions and vocal spiritual exercises. Such minutes of previous meetings as will aid the meeting in determining the nature of the business which should come before it should be read. All the minutes of the previous meeting may or may not be read as the meeting directs.

Minutes are preserved and, for more important meetings, they are printed. A record is thus kept which has become throughout the history of the Society of Friends both a spiritual diary and a chronicle of social action. Gratitude is due to the faithful scribes who have qualified themselves for this important religious service. When, in any meeting, there is a considerable amount of correspondence concerned with such matters as keeping an active list of names and addresses, notifying committee members of the time and place of meetings, aiding committees in implementing their decisions, arranging for lectures or for hospitality for traveling Friends, the meeting may employ a secretary to attend to such current requirements. It is important that such a secretary feel no special responsibility, different from that of other members, in regard to the meeting for worship.

Difficulties and value of this method

As compared with parliamentary procedure this method of conducting a meeting requires more patience and takes more.

time. To succeed fully the members should be bound together by friendship, affection and sympathetic understanding. Factions and chronic differences are serious obstacles. The members should be religiously minded, religion being a powerful solvent of the type of self-centeredness which makes group action difficult. Here the Quaker method differs fundamentally from several other consensus methods. Persons who are dogmatic, who speak with an air of finality or authority and who go to the meeting determined less to find the truth than to win acceptance of their opinions are exceedingly difficult to absorb. The attitude of a debater is out of place. The object is to explore as well as convince.

Questions before the meeting could be decided quickly by taking a vote, but the object is not speed but right decision. Sometimes insight into the one truth accessible to all evolves slowly when many trends of thought interpenetrate. The voting method, depending as it does on quantitative relations, is mechanical, but the Friends' method of attaining results exhibits principles typical of organic growth. The synthesis of a variety of elements is often obtained by a kind of cross-fertilization, and the final result is not therefore, or at least it ought not to be, a compromise. Given time and the proper conditions, a group idea, which is not the arithmetical sum of individual contributions, nor their greatest common divisor, but a new creation or mutation, finally evolves.

When B speaks following A, what B says is a combination of his and A's opinion. C follows and adds his contribution, which would be different had A and B not spoken. Each speaker credits every other speaker with at least some genuine insight. Thus the united judgment is slowly built up until it finds such expression by some individual as can be endorsed by the meeting as a whole. No minority should remain with a feeling of having been over-ridden.

35

Even if it requires years, as was the case when the Society of Friends freed its slaves, this way may still be more expeditious than other methods in producing the right result. A minority can keep a question open in a Quaker meeting whereas, by the acceptance of majority rule, the minority's view might have been out-voted and a wrong decision, very difficult to change or perhaps irrevocable, might have been made. It often happens that neither the majority nor the minority is right, in which case the Quaker way may provide time for the truth to become apparent. There is also another point to be noted; in the voting method of "one man one vote" the opinion of the foolish or indifferent counts for as much as that of the wise, interested or responsible. In the Quaker meeting for business, wise and foolish are both listened to, but the contribution of each to the final judgment has at least an opportunity to be gauged in proportion to its wisdom.

This way is based on religious rather than secular concepts. The members of the group discover experimentally that, as they become united with God, so also do they become united with one another. Unity is always possible because the same Light of Truth shines in some measure in every human heart tending toward the same goal. By prayer, meditation and worship that goal gradually becomes apparent.

Business before the meeting*

• Committees for special and comparatively unimportant purposes are generally appointed by nominations from the floor. Individuals suggest names and, if the person named is present and there is no objection from him or from others,

---

* For further details regarding items in this chapter consult the books of discipline of the various Yearly Meetings.

the name stands. As a rule, members not present should not be appointed. Sometimes attenders who are not members may be asked to serve. In general, the first person named acts as the initial convener. At the committee's first meeting a permanent chairman is agreed upon. The clerk or someone else who is qualified to express a judgment should indicate the appropriate number of committee members. Officials of the meeting such as elders, overseers, clerk, recorder, treasurer, members of standing committees and of other important committees are, in general, nominated by a special nominating committee. The report of this committee is placed before the meeting for approval, at which time new names may be added or names previously suggested may be dropped. Sometimes committees are given the power to co-opt members who have a special knowledge of subjects under consideration.

A Yearly Meeting (or an Association) of Friends usually finds it convenient to empower an executive committee to act for it on matters which cannot be postponed in the intervals when it is not in session. Such a committee has had various names. It was first called the Meeting for Sufferings, having been initiated in order to help Friends in times of persecution. This name still persists in some places, but elsewhere the executive body is variously named the Representative Meeting, the Representative Committee or the Permanent Board. The responsibilities of such a committee should be carefully defined and limited.

Standing committees generally report to the meeting at regular intervals, either orally or in writing.

The business of a committee while in session is conducted by the same methods as is the business of the meeting as a whole, the chairman usually acting as clerk. The session should begin and end with a settled period of silence. It is well for the number of committees to be reduced to a minimum, so that the meeting can, as a whole, feel under the weight of all important matters. Specialization of function, if carried too far, will destroy organic unity. A problem is not disposed of simply by appointing a committee to deal with it.

• *Pastoral Care.* In most meetings shepherding the flock is assigned to the Overseers, though certain duties of this kind have already been described as allocated to those exercising the functions of elders or of members of the Committee on Ministry and Counsel.* Overseers have tended to be at least four in number, men and women, appointed to serve for a definite period. Pastoral care should, however, be the concern of all members of the meeting and individuals who have special concerns regarding it should lay them before the overseers, or the whole business meeting.

Overseers, or their equivalent, are expected to visit all the families in the meeting at least once a year, and oftener in cases of illness, death or special trouble. They should also have a similar care for attenders of the meeting. If a family or individual is in financial need, help should be extended from the funds of the meeting, either by the overseers or by some special committee set up for the purpose. This should be treated as a confidential matter. In special cases a committee or an individual should be appointed to look after a family or individual. If a family needs help or advice regarding such matters as the education of children, or financial affairs generally, the overseers should consider it their duty to extend it or to see that it is otherwise provided. If differences exist between members, overseers should endeavor to see that reconciliation is effected and that arbitrators are appointed if need be. Friends should not go to law with each other. Letters should be written to distant members at least once a

---

* Or "Meeting on Worship and Ministry."

year. If members do not regularly attend meeting, the overseers should look into the situation and if possible correct the condition. If any member is guilty of acts seriously contrary to the principles of the Society of Friends, the overseers should deal with him in a spirit of love for his good as well as for the meeting's reputation. If the case is serious so that by it the Society is brought into disrepute or into a misunderstanding of its position, the matter should be brought before the whole meeting. In extreme cases the meeting may feel it right to disown the member, but only after he has been lovingly dealt with for a long period in a spirit of reconciliation. In modern times disownment seldom occurs. The names of members who have shown no interest in the Society for several years should be dropped from the roll, but only after they have, if possible, been consulted in the matter.

• *Finances.* All money needed for the work of the Monthly, Quarterly and Yearly Meetings is raised by the Monthly Meeting and entrusted to its Treasurer. A committee is usually appointed to suggest to each individual a contribution which, in their opinion, is appropriate to his circumstances and to the need of the meeting. This suggestion is confidential and the member is free to follow his own conscience in the matter. In some meetings no suggestion is made. In similar fashion the higher meetings assess the lower. No collection is taken in the meeting for worship or in any public gathering.

• *Applications for Membership.* Application for membership is made to the Monthly Meeting by letter addressed to the overseers or to the clerk. The meeting, or in some cases the committee of overseers, appoints a committee, usually consisting of two persons, to interview the applicant. It is their duty to ascertain whether or not he understands the beliefs and practices of the Society of Friends and whether or not he is in substantial agreement with them and intends to conduct himself accordingly. They should report their finding and judgment to a future Monthly Meeting. If the meeting grants the application, a minute is made to that effect and the applicant notified. Applications may be made by parents on behalf of minor children. A meeting is usually reluctant to take into membership a person who has not been in attendance at the meeting for worship over a reasonable length of time. This however should not bar persons living at a distance from becoming members.

Specific qualifications for membership do not appear in Yearly Meeting books of discipline. They are largely a matter for Monthly Meeting judgment. As Monthly Meetings differ considerably among themselves, different standards for membership exist.

The procedure for resignation is similar to the procedure for application. A committee is appointed and the matter is brought up at the next Monthly Meeting.

There was no regularly enrolled membership in the Society of Friends until 1737. Before that time and for a while after, attendance at the Business Meeting was on invitation. The habit Friends had formed of looking after those of their group who were in "necessitous circumstances" made it necessary to have a list of those who were entitled to material help. Thus an enrolled membership came into being. This list naturally included children as well as adults, for children were even more in need of such help. Hence arose birthright membership, the custom of enrolling as members the children of members. This custom still largely prevails. It is based on the conception of a meeting as a community similar in type to a family. Children are welcomed into the religious community for the same reason that they are welcomed into a family and they come therefore, from the very beginning, under the care and oversight of the meeting.

• *Traveling in the Ministry.* If, according to the traditional phrase, a member wishes to "travel in the service of Truth," visiting meetings and Friends in distant parts, his concern should be laid before his Monthly Meeting for its consideration. For wider service the Quarterly or Yearly Meeting should also be consulted if time permits. If the meeting approves he should be granted a minute expressing the unity of the meeting with his concern. This minute should be presented to the meetings to which he goes. It is customary, where practicable, for traveling Friends to be welcomed into the homes of those whom they visit. This has the double advantage of saving expense to the traveler and of extending more intimately the benefit of his visit. It is usual for ministers not to travel singly but with a suitable companion appointed by the meeting. Special meetings may be appointed by overseers if the visitor so desires. At the conclusion of his service the minute should be returned and a report made to the meeting. The meeting should see to it that such service is not hindered by lack of personal funds.

• *Outreach to Neighbors and People in General.* The Monthly Meeting should not be exclusively concerned for its own members. It should be sensitive to the needs of its neighborhood and to the larger population around it. The services which such a group may render are numerous and changing from generation to generation if not from decade to decade. Education is a continuous responsibility. Tensions, racial, economic, and political, frequently require alleviation. Facilities for health and recreation need to be developed. Local responsibility for civic, state, national and international matters lags unless all citizens take their proper part in its maintenance. Social evils of many sorts call for alert attention. Cooperation should be extended to established social agencies which can inform the meeting of special services that it can render. Work camps may be established to enable younger members to take part in special remedial activities. The interest which the meeting's members take in the business of the Monthly Meeting will largely depend upon the variety and validity of the activities engaged in and reported upon.

It is important that the meeting occasionally take into account places at which a new meeting ought to be set up and the means which may be used to help in starting such a meeting. New meetings may begin with a very small nucleus of concerned persons. Once such a meeting is inaugurated it should receive the loving care of the parent meeting whose members should regularly visit it according to some prearranged plan. Old meetings from which Friends have moved to other localities should not be lost sight of. Frequently they can be revived or revitalized to the distinct benefit of the neighborhood.

Other business

• *Records* of membership, of removals to and from other meetings and of births, deaths and marriages should be accurately kept. A special recorder or secretary should be appointed for this service. He should forward to the superior meetings such vital statistics as are asked for. Such a recorder may also be asked to keep an up-to-date list of names and addresses of attenders and of persons to whom should be sent announcements of meeting events. He or she should also see to it that such announcements are duly sent. In some cases these duties are performed by an employed meeting secretary.

• *Certificates of Removal* may be granted to members wishing to remove their membership to another meeting. These serve as credentials as well as letters of introduction and recommend such persons as can be recommended to the Christian care and oversight of the meeting to which they go. The meeting to which the certificate is sent is under no obligation to receive such persons into membership and should make careful inquiries regarding them before accepting them. Friends removing their residence to the neighborhood of another meeting, but not wishing to transfer their membership, should be granted simply a letter of introduction or a sojourning minute to the meeting within the confines of which they intend to reside. The meeting may then grant them the full privileges of members. For the better conduct of business and to strengthen the sense of local responsibility, Friends are encouraged to have their official membership recorded in the meeting which they attend. Requests for the transfer of membership should first come to the attention of overseers.

• Marriages of members or of others wishing to be married after the manner of Friends, are under the care and subject to the approval of the Monthly Meeting, preferably that of which the bride is a member. When the meeting is informed of the intention of the persons concerned, a committee is appointed to make sure that no obstructions appear. If the man is a member of another meeting, it should appoint a similar committee of inquiry. In the case of the marriage of a member to a non-member or of two non-members, state laws should be consulted. When the reports of clearness are received, the meeting in charge of the wedding appoints a committee of oversight to see that all legal requirements are complied with and necessary facts recorded and that the marriage is properly performed at a regular meeting for worship or one appointed especially for the purpose. This committee should encourage simplicity at both ceremony and reception. The marriage ceremony is carried through by the contracting parties without the aid of an officiating minister. The union of man and woman in marriage being an act of God rather than of man, it cannot be consummated by any person appointed for this service.

The following is a typical form of procedure for a Quaker wedding. After the meeting is well settled, those in attendance having been placed by the ushers in appropriate seats, the bride and groom enter, arm in arm, followed by the wedding party (if any), and take their seats on a facing bench. Sometimes the wedding party also sits on the facing bench. According to an older custom, the groom's parents sit by him and the bride's parents sit by her, facing the meeting. After about five minutes of silence the bride and groom rise and, taking each other by the hand, repeat the wedding ceremony. This ceremony permits minor variations. In its usual form the groom says, "In the presence of God and of this assembly (or—and before these, our friends) I take thee, (name of bride), to be my wife, promising with Divine assistance to be unto thee a loving and faithful husband as long as we both shall live." The bride then says the same thing with the necessary changes of name and of "wife" to "husband." The ushers immediately bring forward on a table the marriage certificate which is signed by the contracting parties, the bride signing her new name. This certificate which contains the words of the promises which the bride and groom have made to each other is then read aloud by some person appointed for this service. A meeting for worship follows which is held according to the same principles as any other meeting for worship, the silence being occasionally broken by those who have some message to give, perhaps a message of love and encouragement to the newly wedded pair.

After the meeting, perhaps at a reception held elsewhere, the certificate is signed by all of the guests who were witnesses to the marriage. The usual form of the marriage certificate can be found in Yearly Meeting Books of Discipline which should be consulted also for other details. An engraved certificate can be secured at 1515 Cherry Street, Philadelphia, or at 302 Arch Street, Philadelphia.

• *Funerals* or memorial meetings, whether held at a meeting house or elsewhere, are conducted according to the principles which govern a Friends' meeting for worship. Speaking in such a meeting is based upon the same considerations. Such speaking frequently takes the form of an appreciation of the life and work of the deceased. In all matters pertaining to burial, simplicity is urged. It is in line with current interpretation of this advice that memorial meetings are tending to take the place of the type of funeral in which the body of the deceased is present. Interment or cremation is, in such a case, private.

The Queries

In early times the Yearly Meeting sent down to its constituent meetings a series of questions in order that by their answers it might keep informed upon such matters as the regularity of holding meetings, the condition of Friends suffering persecution, "the spread of the Truth," and other pertinent facts. In the course of time the Queries increased in number and complexity until they included questions regarding all the important religious and social testimonies of Friends. As such they became a means of self-examination and evaluation as well as a way of informing the higher meeting of the condition of its constituent meetings. The Queries have never been concerned with theological opinions but only with behavior.

Most meetings today have kept the Queries as a kind of Quaker confessional and some Yearly Meetings still maintain the once universal practice of sending written answers. The Queries are read and spoken to in the business meeting once a year, individual queries being considered at different times. The clerk generally records in his minutes a summary of remarks made during this self-evaluation. The Queries are also sometimes read immediately after the meeting for worship to remind Friends of the standard of behavior which they have set for themselves. These Queries in various forms can be found in Yearly Meeting disciplines. Some independent meetings have adopted formulations of their own.

The Queries have frequently been revised. The following twelve Queries of Philadelphia Yearly Meeting were adopted in 1947. They are based largely on earlier Queries with some alterations and additions. The division into twelve Queries permits one of these Queries to be considered at each of the twelve Monthly Meetings during the year and the division into four groups permits one of these groups to be considered at each of the four Quarterly Meetings during the year. The reports sent to the Yearly Meeting by the Quarterly Meetings are based on a consideration of the Queries and sometimes also on written answers to them. These Queries can be reduced to four by using only the headings of the four groups.

The Philadelphia Queries

I. WHAT IS THE STATE OF YOUR MEETINGS FOR WORSHIP AND BUSINESS?

1. *Religious Meetings*

Are your meetings for worship and business held in expectant waiting for divine guidance?

Is there a living silence in which you feel drawn together by the power of God in your midst?

Do your meetings give evidence that Friends come to them with hearts and minds prepared for worship?

Are your meetings a source of strength and guidance for daily Christian living?

2. *Ministry*

Is the vocal ministry in your meetings exercised under the direct leading of the Holy Spirit, without prearrangement, and in the simplicity and sincerity of Truth?

46

Do you foster the use and growth of the spiritual gifts of your members?

3. *Participation in Meeting*

Do your resident members attend meetings regularly and punctually?

To what extent are your meetings for worship attended by persons not in membership and are they welcomed and encouraged to continue attendance?

Are your meetings for business held in a spirit of love, understanding and forbearance, and do you seek the right course of action in humble submission to the authority of Truth and patient search for unity?

II. HOW DO FRIENDS CARE FOR ONE ANOTHER?

4. *Unity within the Meeting*

Are love and unity maintained among you?

Do you manifest a forgiving spirit and a care for the reputation of others?

When differences arise, are endeavors made to settle them speedily and in a spirit of meekness and love?

5. *Education*

Do your children receive the loving care of the Meeting and are they brought under such influences as tend to develop their religious life?

What efforts are you making to educate all your members in the knowledge of the Bible, of Christianity and of the history and principles of Friends?

Do you maintain schools for the education of your youth under the care of teachers of Christian character in sympathy with the principles of Friends and supervised by committees of the Meeting?

Do you encourage members to send their children to Friends' schools and do you give such financial aid as may be necessary?

6. *Oversight of the Membership*

What is being done to draw members together into a spirit of fellowship?

Does the Meeting keep in contact, either by visits or personal letters, with all its members?

Are Friends in material need assisted as their circumstances require?

Do you counsel with those whose conduct or manner of living gives ground for concern?

III. HOW DO FRIENDS MEET THEIR RESPONSIBILITIES OUTSIDE THE MEETING?

7. *Social and Economic Relationships*

What are you doing as individuals or as a Meeting:

To aid those in need of material help?

To encourage total abstinence and remove the causes of intemperance?

To insure equal opportunities in social and economic life for those who suffer discrimination because of race, creed or social class?

To create a social and economic system which will so function as to sustain and enrich life for all?

8. *Civic Responsibility*

What are you doing as individuals or as a Meeting:

To understand and remove the causes of war and develop the conditions and institutions of peace?

To carry your share of responsibilities in the government of your community, state and nation, and to assure freedom of speech, and of religion and equal educational opportunities for all?

9. *Extending Our Message*

What are you doing as individuals or as a Meeting:

To interpret to others the message of Friends and to cooperate with others in spreading the Christian message?

IV. TO WHAT EXTENT IS YOUR PERSONAL LIFE IN ACCORD WITH OUR PRINCIPLES?

10. *The Home*

Do you make a place in your daily life for inward retirement and communion with the Divine Spirit?

Do you make your home a place where friendship, peace, and

refreshment of spirit are found, and do you have regular periods of family worship?

Do you frequently and reverently read the Bible and other religious literature?

Do you choose those recreations which will strengthen your physical, mental, and spiritual life and avoid those that may prove a hindrance to yourself and others?

11. *Self-Discipline*

Do you keep to simplicity and moderation in your speech, your manner of living, and your pursuit of business?

Are you careful to keep your business and your outward activities from absorbing time and energy that should be given to spiritual growth and the service of your religious society?

Are you punctual in keeping promises, just in the payment of debts, and honorable in all your dealings?

Are you free from the use of judicial oaths, from betting and gambling and from practices based on the principles of gambling?

Are you free from the use and handling of intoxicants and narcotic drugs?

Do you take your right share of responsibility in work and service for the Meeting?

12. *Human Brotherhood*

Do you live in the life and power which takes away the occasion of all wars? Do you seek to take your part in the ministry of reconciliation between individuals, groups, and nations? Do you faithfully maintain our testimony against military training and other preparation for war and against participation in war as inconsistent with the spirit and teaching of Christ?

In all your relations with others do you treat them as brothers and equals?

The ministry of teaching

Since the religion of the Society of Friends is based on an inward experience deeper than intellectual concepts, it cannot be taught in the same way that subjects are taught in a school curriculum. Religion of this type is communicated only through itself. If a child observes sincere religious acts performed by his elders he becomes thereby religiously educated. There is only one Teacher of religion, the Divine Spirit working in the heart, either directly or through others. The meeting for worship and the meeting for business are therefore the chief religious educational agencies in the Society of Friends.

• *First Day* (or Sunday) *Schools* did not exist among Friends until comparatively recent times. They were objected to on the ground of resemblance to programmed religious services. Such Bible teaching as was approved in schools took place through a weekly exercise in committing Bible verses to memory. Today Friends have, for the most part, adopted the usual form of Bible teaching which characterizes the average Protestant Sunday School. Here the methods of overcoming illiteracy in religious and moral matters closely resemble the methods used in other types of schools.

Many important facts about religion can be communicated by the usual pedagogical methods. Every adult, as well as every child, should become fully aware of his cultural heritage as transmitted through a study of the Bible, of the history of religion, of the history of the Christian Church and of the Society of Friends. Such information is not only essential to every well educated Friend, making him more effectual in any service which he may undertake, but it also often opens the door to deeper and more direct religious knowledge. To become aware that one is part of a great stream of religious thought and experience flowing out of the remote past into the future is a necessary prerequisite to attaining insight into the problems of the present.

• *The Bible* must be taught, especially as it furnishes the language and figures of speech in which religious experience is usually expressed in the West. Friends' First Day Schools tend to emphasize those particular moral issues which are of greatest interest to the Society, such, for instance, as the need for peace and understanding among races, nations, and classes. These schools usually undertake also to teach the history and doctrines of the Society of Friends.

• *The Adult Discussion Group* may be a part of the First Day School program or it may meet on a week day at some member's home. It exhibits nothing peculiar to Quaker practice. Such a group meets under a leader to consider topics of current interest and to pool information (or ignorance) about them. As a rule it is concerned with the education of opinion rather than with action. If action is aimed at, the group should resolve itself into a Quaker business meeting and operate on the principles of such a meeting.

Much depends on the leader. It is a fortunate group in which the convener is more interested in drawing out the opinions of others than in expressing his own. The subject is usually introduced by some qualified person appointed in advance to outline the main problems and facts which everyone should know in order to take an intelligent part in the discussion. The leader may begin the discussion by asking a pertinent question. The best leader is one who is the most skillful in asking questions of the group or of individuals at appropriate times. He should not be afraid of occasional periods of silence when the members can reflect upon the problem before them. He should see that terms used loosely are precisely defined, realizing that differences of opinion are sometimes due solely to differing interpretations of words. He should encourage those who are hesitant in expressing their views and restrain those who tend to monopolize the time. At the end he should summarize the discussion and conclusions, if any. Questions which come up requiring information not possessed by any member should be referred to someone for an investigation resulting in a report at a future meeting. If the group desires, a secretary may be appointed to keep a record of the discussion to be read at the

51

close of the meeting. A Friends' discussion should begin and end with a brief period of silence.

The most useful function of a discussion group is to stimulate the reading of important books. If such books are read by the whole group and considered chapter by chapter at successive meetings, greater benefit can be derived from them than would be obtained by solitary perusal.

• *Lectures* should occasionally be arranged by the Monthly Meeting for the enlightenment of its members and of others. Such lectures are sometimes given following the meeting for business, but care must be taken that the business of the meeting is not hurried or set aside because of lectures. Monthly Meetings should arrange to hear the leaders in their local communities. Religious, political, educational, and industrial leaders should be heard, the latter including both employers and employees.

• *Schools* were set up by many Monthly Meetings as the Quaker movement spread in the 17th and 18th centuries throughout the American colonies. The teachers were concerned Friends if such could be secured and the pupils went regularly to the midweek morning meeting. The day's session generally began and closed with a brief period of Bible reading followed by a solemn pause. With the coming of public schools early in the 19th century the number of Friends' elementary schools rapidly declined. At the same time, boarding schools and academies were established with a more specific program for surrounding the pupils with such religious influences as would fit them for the duties of active members of the Religious Society of Friends. A generation or two later a few of these schools became colleges. Other Quaker colleges were founded as such.

The Quaker day school or boarding school was throughout closely integrated with the meeting. The object was not to equip the pupils for success according to worldly standards but to prepare them to fit into a special type of community life lived according to the Quaker pattern. As this pattern of living has tended to lose its peculiar aspects and to approximate the general social pattern, many modern Friends' schools and colleges have tended in various degrees to resemble other institutions in character and objectives.

• *The Conference* has, within the present century, become an important type of adult educational effort in the Society of Friends. Unlike the Yearly Meeting, the conference has no legislative powers. Its program consists of meetings for worship, lectures, and discussions. One object of the conference is to promote acquaintance and understanding among various groups of Friends who might not otherwise meet together. It attempts to aid thinking and may even formulate its own conclusions regarding some important problem facing the Society of Friends or the world at large. In such an attempt experts in various related fields may be called in to speak. Each day of the conference should begin with a period of worship. If the conference is large it should, for at least a part of the time, be divided into smaller groups both for worship and discussion.

• *Adult Education* is of peculiar significance in the Society of Friends because of the important duties which are shared by all its members rather than, as in other religious societies, laid upon specialists trained in theological schools. The first systematic adult education specifically intended to fit Friends for their peculiar responsibilities was undertaken at the Woodbrooke Settlement, in England, which was founded in 1903. Short summer schools in America began at Haverford and Swarthmore early in the twentieth century. From 1917 to 1927 the Woolman School at Swarthmore and the T. Wistar Brown School at Haverford offered longer and more advanced courses in religious and social subjects. These efforts now largely focus at Pendle Hill, Wallingford, Pennsylvania, which was opened in 1930 as a center for religious and social study. At Pendle Hill many of the practices outlined in this book are integrated with the educational program in such a way as to constitute a training in the Quaker way of life. Pendle Hill is also used as a center for training persons for foreign work under the American Friends Service Committee. Adult education is undertaken by the American Friends Service Committee through summer institutes and through work camps.

In these various types of education it should be noted that Friends have always had a testimony against what might be called verbalism, that is an undue emphasis on an expert use of language rather than on the substance of which the words are symbols. This testimony is as important in the ministry of teaching as in the ministry of the meeting for worship.

• *The Social Life of the Meeting* should be a concern of the Monthly Meeting as a whole. The result both of the meeting for worship and the meeting for business depends to a large degree on the inter-play of understanding, friendship and love among the members. The meeting should gather socially from time to time as may be arranged by the overseers or by special committees. Monthly Meetings may be followed or preceded by a common meal. Attenders as well as members should be invited to such social occasions. Sometimes a meeting should combine for such an interest with another not too distant meeting. Occasionally young people may arrange separate social gatherings but in general it is better that the meeting's social life resemble a large family with all ages present.

The meeting membership should not become so exclusively unified along social and religious lines that outsiders, who become convinced of the principles of the Society of Friends, may hesitate to try to gain entrance to it. A meeting is particularly fortunate if it contains representatives of more than one race or economic class. Such variety widens its mental horizon. When a meeting succeeds in making persons of various nations, races, callings, educational opportunities and

54

economic status feel genuinely at home it has come a long way toward the realization of that gospel in which there is "neither Jew nor Greek, bond nor free."

Social testimonies

So far we have been concerned largely with activities within the meeting. The emphasis has been placed on the means of creating changes for the better within the individual and within the specific groups. Experience shows that, as the individual becomes more sensitive, or, to use the old Quaker word, more "tender" to the movings of the Divine Spirit, this sensitivity finds its outward expression not simply within the group itself but also in widening circles outside. Divine-human bonds produce inter-human bonds. Man should begin the reformation of society in that area where his most immediate responsibility lies, that is in himself, and work from there outward as the way opens.

But, though this process of beginning with the individual is primary, there is a secondary process in the opposite direction which must not be neglected. Structural changes in society have an educational effect in producing changes in the individual. Thus, if a meeting acts according to a certain pattern of behavior, the individual member becomes educated in that pattern and tends to adopt it as his own. Similarly in society at large, good laws and good institutions tend to produce good individuals. But this process is secondary because good laws cannot be enforced, except by violence, if they are too far beyond the standards of a large proportion of the individuals concerned. Hence those who believe in peaceful methods will place the first emphasis on inward convincement. Religion has always been the most important means in human history of producing changes from within.

Activities of Friends on behalf of others have usually been motivated by a desire for clearness of conscience. A social condition becomes a matter of concern if it gives rise to a feeling of inward spiritual discomfort. Such concerns do not originate externally through human appointment, but inwardly through a feeling that God has laid a burden upon the bearer. If the Friend with an uneasy conscience cannot remedy the matter himself he can secure a measure of inward satisfaction by doing what he feels called upon to do regardless of results in terms of success or failure. In appealing to wrongdoers the Quaker appeal has generally been based, not so much on the physical harm such persons were doing to others, for physical harm is comparatively unimportant, as on the spiritual harm they were doing to themselves and the resulting loss of inward peace.

The Society of Friends has never put forth a blueprint of the structure of an ideal society, having the same reluctance in this respect as in putting forth a religious creed. Nevertheless the meeting itself should aim, however short it may come of attaining its ideal, at a pattern of human relations between its own members which could be considered as ideal for society as a whole.

This ideal pattern should be incarnated in the meeting as a social unit in which the various parts are organically related so that the "entire body is welded together and compacted by every joint with which it is supplied, the due activity of each part enables the Body to grow and build itself up in love." Eph. 4: 16, Moffatt's translation). As such an organism, the meeting becomes in some degree the "mystical body of Christ," to use an ancient Christian phrase, and the continuation of His incarnation. It becomes the feet and hands through which His work is carried on in the world.

From another point of view the meeting becomes both a laboratory and a training ground for a better social order.

All the social doctrines of Friends are first practiced within the meeting where the environment is favorable. Those who have learned these lessons in such a seed-bed can there become strong enough and resourceful enough to continue similar practices in the world outside.

Every social testimony of Friends goes through a process of discovery and development. It takes time to realize the social implications of a religious position. For example, the New Testament does not condemn slavery though it enunciates principles which eventually did away with slavery in Europe. The Society of Friends is still very far from having discovered all the consequences of its religious premises.

At the price of over-simplification, let us outline the Quaker social doctrines under four heads—community, harmony, equality, and simplicity. Obviously the four overlap, being derived out of the same fundamental principle.

• *Community* within the meeting becomes manifest as an attempt of the members to share with one another, spiritually, intellectually, socially, and economically. Outside the meeting it is manifest in attempts to increase the harmonious interdependence of men everywhere, in order to reduce self-centeredness and conflict. Friends have frequently made efforts to aid the poor and weak and to improve the condition of depressed classes. Once this took place largely through philanthropy in the narrower sense of that word, but many today favor methods which attack the causes rather than the results of social evils. In addition to emphasizing the importance of professional social work in areas where expert knowledge is required, Friends especially stress individual responsibility on the part of all persons. There is a relationship between this emphasis and the Quaker insistence upon the religious responsibility of all members which has produced the non-professional ministry. Friends encourage the kind of social service in which the work is done *with* rather

57

than for those who are helped. The summer work camps of the American Friends Service Committee, established as they often are in conflict areas, and the shorter term week-end camps of the Philadelphia Yearly Meetings' Social Order Committee are specific examples of this kind of effort.

During every war since the beginning of its history, the Society of Friends has engaged in some kind of relief and reconstruction work for those who have suffered devastation, hunger, or pestilence. This relief work has, when its nature made it possible, been characterized by the same principle of working along with a population rather than for them. For example, in France after the First World War, Quaker relief workers worked with the peasants in their fields, and in Germany they supplied food for children in cooperation with the German social agencies.

One can envisage a meeting in which this principle of community is developed to such an extent that the members share with each other economically to the same degree that they share intellectually and spiritually. Such sharing normally occurs in an average family, and the tendency is therefore, to that extent, present in our cultural inheritance. But the family is too small a unit to give the kind of security needed today. The tiny unit is too readily swept away in an economic storm. A religious family, being larger, could have greater stability. In most Friends' meetings members in need are cared for by the meeting as a whole.

• Harmony is used here instead of pacifism, the latter word having come to mean, for many persons, simply an unwillingness to take part in war. The word pacifism or its equivalent does not occur in Quaker writings until recently because the peace testimony was once so intimately a part of the Quakers' way of life that they did not set it by itself in a special category. The word harmony is used here to designate the function which any part exerts in an integrated whole. This function is such that no part of the social organism imposes violence on any other part, but all work together in harmony. Those who hold the peace testimony seek to reconcile all individuals to one another so that a society will exist in which cooperation supplants conflict. We can, in the last resort, find no better term for this effort than the Biblical phrase, "the ministry of reconciliation."

Such positive pacifism within a Friends' meeting implies the ability of the members to achieve unity without authoritarian compulsion exercised by an individual, a majority, a program, a ritual, or a creed. The methods for attaining this type of unity are described in detail above. These methods can, in some degree, be applied to the settlement of disputes in the world at large. A settlement so reached does not result from one party prevailing over the other. Each contributes to the final outcome, even though it may show that one side or the other is totally wrong.

From this ultimate aim of reconciliation arises the peace testimony in the narrower sense. Quakers cannot engage in war as a method of settling international disputes, for war is a test of strength, not a search for truth and justice. The methods used depart so far from ideal procedures that the attainment of truth and justice is highly improbable. Only spiritual means can achieve a spiritual end. Quakers are fighters, but they use weapons that they believe will really attain the results aimed at, however long a time it may take. But the religious pacifist does not base his position solely on the apparently better results achieved by pacific methods since no human being can foresee what all the results of any action will be in the long course of history. Quaker pacifism is based primarily on religious insight which often gives clear indication that certain actions are wrong irrespective of the results which may be humanly foreseen. The character of the source of action and the moral quality of the will which acts are generally more evident to a highly sensitive person than uncertain consequences in a distant future. Every one must live up to his own conscience which reveals to him the highest moral values that he knows, whether this conscience leads him to fight or to refrain from fighting. Experience shows, however, that, in proportion as conscience becomes educated and sensitized through prayer and worship, men will more and more be led to seek that type of solution to differences which leads away from violence toward peaceable reconciliation.

The Quaker also believes that in refusing to take part in war he is following the injunctions of the Founder of the Christian religion. He finds by experience that the Christ within and the Christ of history speak with the same voice. The Christian is "in the world but not of it" in the sense that the code of that Divine Kingdom, to which he aspires to belong, is not the code of the world around him.

Opinions differ on how far this opposition to the use of violence in dealing with human beings can be carried into situations other than international war. Friends generally consider the use of police power permissible when exercised impartially in seeking to preserve the rights of the criminal as well as of society. But even here non-violent methods can be more successful than most persons suppose. Friends have been active in prison reform, believing that punishment should never be exercised to wreak vengeance on the wrongdoer but rather to reform him. They oppose capital punishment. They were probably the first to use non-violent methods in dealing with the insane. An early reform abolished corporal punishment in Friends' schools. That Friends have been pioneers in methods now universally used in dealing with prisoners, the mentally ill, and children may show that their opposition to war indicates a similar trend in pioneering for the future.

• *Equality*, expressed as a Quaker social testimony, means that all men have equal worth in the sight of God and that their personalities must be held equally inviolate. This does not mean that all men are of equal ability. In a Friends' business meeting, for instance, some members have more weight than others. It means rather that distinctions arising from sex, race, economic status, nationality, and education are unimportant and should never be used either to flatter or humiliate.

Equality in the ministry between men and women was recognized in the Society of Friends from the beginning. Equality was the earliest social testimony. Even before all Friends recognized the pacifist implications of their religion, a number were dismissed from Cromwell's army because they treated their officers as social equals.

Under this head, perhaps, can be placed the long and painful struggle which resulted in placing all religious affiliations on an equality before the civil law. Friends in England in the 17th century refused to obey the laws which forbade non-conformist sects to worship according to their consciences and as a result many thousands were cast into prison where many died. Still more lost all their property through fines. The coming of religious liberty to England was a great triumph of non-violent methods after the then usual method of violence had failed. Only in those American colonies which were controlled politically by the Quakers, namely Pennsylvania, New Jersey, Rhode Island, and Delaware was there no state church. In this respect, as well as in others, Quaker tradition, especially as embodied in the constitution of Pennsylvania, exercised a powerful influence on the Constitution of the United States.

The full implications of the doctrine of racial equality developed more slowly. Friends freed their slaves a century before the Civil War. They have from the beginning been active in educating Negroes and Indians. Some Yearly Meetings maintain race-relations committees which seek opportunities to promote inter-racial understanding. Work in line with this testimony has failed to keep pace with the need.

The doctrine of equality as far as it refers to economic status is, as yet, largely undeveloped. Small beginnings have been made. Servants in Quaker households have often received the same social consideration as members of the family and in the meeting they have sometimes had more influence than their employers. There are instances of Quaker business men giving unusual privileges and responsibilities to their employees. From time to time Pendle Hill, or a committee on the social order, brings employers and representatives of employees together to discuss their common problems. Many Friends today are groping for light on these difficult questions which are rendered even more complex by contemporary conditions.

• *Simplicity* is a testimony which has assumed many different forms. It means in general—sincerity, genuineness, avoidance of superfluity. It has been commonly referred to in books of discipline as "simplicity in dress, speech, and behavior," or an equivalent phrase.

In *dress*, simplicity first led to dispensing with useless ornaments at a time when the dress of the fashionable was excessively elaborate. Finding themselves victimized by changes in fashion which benefited no one but the tailor, Friends adopted one fashion and clung to it for more than a hundred years. This became known as the "plain dress." As such it was a means by which the wearer could inform the world where he stood. This dress has now largely disappeared. Much ornamentation is still considered out of place. Here, simplicity and modern good taste coincide.

In *speech*, simplicity means that the truth should be stated as simply as possible without affectation, excess words or rhetorical flourish. As a result, directness and often bluntness became characteristic of Quaker conversation. The Quaker shop-keeper was the first to introduce the one-price system in selling goods. He believed it appropriate to tell at the outset the truth regarding the price he would accept instead of going through the customary drama of bargaining. This turned out to be good business as well as good ethics.

Under simplicity in language should be included the testimony against judicial oaths which imply a double standard of speech, one for the court of justice and the other for less formal occasions. Another reason for the refusal to swear was the express instruction by Jesus. This testimony caused much acute suffering until Friends won the right to make a simple affirmation instead of taking the oath. Today this doctrine has appeared in an entirely new form. Some Friends have lost their positions because of refusal to take an oath of loyalty. While the words they are asked to say express the truth regarding themselves, they consider this requirement to be an entering wedge in a control of opinion characteristic of the police state.

The so-called "plain language," in the more formal sense, refers to the Quaker practice of using to one person the singular pronoun "thou," which in common speech has been replaced by "thee," of omitting the titles Mr. and Mrs., and of numbering the days of the week and the months of the year instead of using names derived from pagan mythology. Discriminations formerly in vogue having largely disappeared today, this aspect of the testimony for simplicity has become meaningless, though many still consider it valuable as a sign of intimacy and religious fellowship.

In behavior, simplicity means avoiding pretense or affectation. On account of a keen interest in decorum, the actions of Friends on social occasions were often characterized by a peculiar grace and dignity which, however, bore little relation to the standardized manners of their day. Simplicity in behavior also means the omission of superfluous activities which serve no good end.

Friends are warned in their books of discipline against "engaging in business beyond their ability to manage." In Quaker journals there are many instances recorded of Friends giving up large businesses in order to engage in smaller ones because the large business took up time and attention that should be given to religious matters. Some Friends have restricted scientific researches for the same reason.

In outlining these social testimonies, it does not need to be pointed out that members of the Society of Friends are far from living up to what they profess. They believe, however, that a high goal is better than a low one and that it is better to aim at the highest and fail than to make a virtue of compromise.

Friends know that they are an integral part of the society in which they live and that they share in its weakness and guilt. They also realize that they have themselves so lived that they are partly responsible for war, for the exploitation of the weak, and for other social evils by which they have materially benefited. Therefore they should be humble and penitent. Yet they believe also in the power of God which can enable men, as George Fox expressed it, to "get atop of" these things.

The early Friends, like the early Christians, did not try to adjust themselves to the world. Their effort was directed toward adjusting the world and themselves to the standards of their religion. The practices outlined here are not now prevalent in the world. They characterize a community of persons which seeks, however much it may fail, to obey the scriptural injunction "Be not conformed to this world but be ye transformed by the renewing of your mind."